Harriet Tubman

Leader of the Underground Railroad

Colonial Leaders

Lord Baltimore
English Politician and Colonist

Benjamin Banneker
American Mathematician and Astronomer

Sir William Berkeley
Governor of Virginia

William Bradford
Governor of Plymouth Colony

Jonathan Edwards
Colonial Religious Leader

Benjamin Franklin
American Statesman, Scientist, and Writer

Anne Hutchinson
Religious Leader

Cotton Mather
Author, Clergyman, and Scholar

Increase Mather
Clergyman and Scholar

James Oglethorpe
Humanitarian and Soldier

William Penn
Founder of Democracy

Sir Walter Raleigh
English Explorer and Author

Caesar Rodney
American Patriot

John Smith
English Explorer and Colonist

Miles Standish
Plymouth Colony Leader

Peter Stuyvesant
Dutch Military Leader

George Whitefield
Clergyman and Scholar

Roger Williams
Founder of Rhode Island

John Winthrop
Politician and Statesman

John Peter Zenger
Free Press Advocate

Revolutionary War Leaders

John Adams
Second U.S. President

Ethan Allen
Revolutionary Hero

Benedict Arnold
Traitor to the Cause

King George III
English Monarch

Nathanael Greene
Military Leader

Nathan Hale
Revolutionary Hero

Alexander Hamilton
First U.S. Secretary of the Treasury

John Hancock
President of the Continental Congress

Patrick Henry
American Statesman and Speaker

John Jay
First Chief Justice of the Supreme Court

Thomas Jefferson
Author of the Declaration of Independence

John Paul Jones
Father of the U.S. Navy

Lafayette
French Freedom Fighter

James Madison
Father of the Constitution

Francis Marion
The Swamp Fox

James Monroe
American Statesman

Thomas Paine
Political Writer

Paul Revere
American Patriot

Betsy Ross
American Patriot

George Washington
First U.S. President

Famous Figures of the Civil War Era

Jefferson Davis
Confederate President

Frederick Douglass
Abolitionist and Author

Ulysses S. Grant
Military Leader and President

Stonewall Jackson
Confederate General

Robert E. Lee
Confederate General

Abraham Lincoln
Civil War President

William Sherman
Union General

Harriet Beecher Stowe
Author of Uncle Tom's Cabin

Sojourner Truth
Abolitionist, Suffragist, and Preacher

Harriet Tubman
Leader of the Underground Railroad

Harriet Tubman

Leader of the Underground Railroad

Norma Jean Lutz

Arthur M. Schlesinger, jr.
Senior Consulting Editor

Chelsea House Publishers

Philadelphia

Produced by 21st Century Publishing and Communications, Inc.
New York, NY. http://www.21cpc.com

CHELSEA HOUSE PUBLISHERS
Production Manager Pamela Loos
Art Director Sara Davis
Director of Photography Judy L. Hasday
Managing Editor James D. Gallagher
Senior Production Editor J. Christopher Higgins

Staff for *HARRIET TUBMAN*
Project Editor Anne Hill
Associate Art Director Takeshi Takahashi
Series Design Keith Trego

The Chelsea House World Wide Web address is
http://www.chelseahouse.com

First Printing
1 3 5 7 9 8 6 4 2

Library of Congress Cataloging-in-Publication Data

Lutz, Norma Jean.
  Harriet Tubman / Norma Jean Lutz.
    p. cm. — (Famous figures of the Civil War era)
  Includes bibliographical references and index.
  ISBN 0–7910–6008–X — ISBN 0–7910–6146–9 (pbk.)
    1. Tubman, Harriet, 1820?–1913—Juvenile literature.
2. Slaves—United States—Biography—Juvenile literature. 3. Afro-
American women—Biography—Juvenile literature. 4. Afro-Americans—
Biography—Juvenile literature. 5. Underground railroad—Juvenile
literature. [1. Tubman, Harriet, 1820?–1913. 2. Slaves. 3. Afro-Americans—
Biography. 4. Women—Biography. 5. Underground railroad.] I. Title.
II. Famous figures of the Civil War era.

E444.T82 L88   2000
305.5'67'092—dc21   00-038389
[B]   CIP

Publisher's Note: In Colonial, Revolutionary War, and Civil War Era
America, there were no standard rules for spelling, punctuation,
capitalization, or grammar. Some of the quotations that appear in
the Colonial Leaders, Revolutionary War Leaders, and Famous
Figures of the Civil War Era series come from original documents
and letters written during this time in history. Original quotations
reflect writing inconsistencies of the period.

Contents

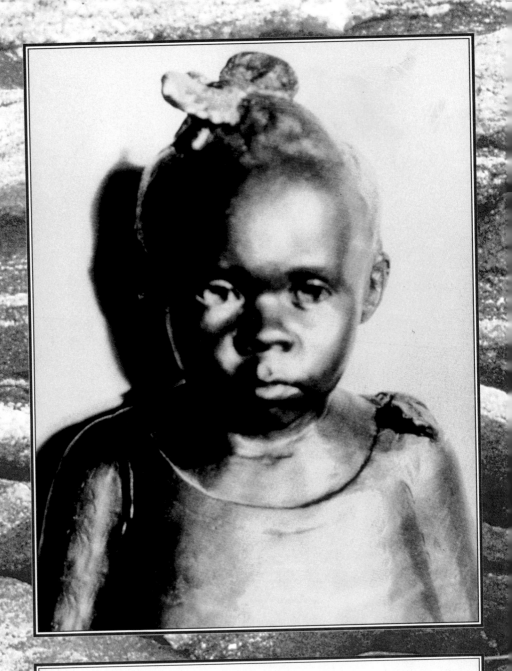

Harriet Tubman was born a slave, like the little girl portrayed in this statue. Harriet had loving parents, whom she later rescued from slavery.

The Slave Girl

Around the year 1820, two slaves had a baby girl. She was their 11th child. They named her Araminta, but everyone called her Minty. Later, she took on her mother's name of Harriet.

Little Harriet's parents were Benjamin Ross and Harriet Green. People called them Old Ben and Old Rit. Their parents had been brought from Africa to America in chains. Old Ben and Old Rit worked at the **plantation** of Edward Brodas, which sat near the Big Buckwater River in Maryland. The plantation produced apples, wheat, rye, and corn. Acres of trees provided timber for building ships in Baltimore, a city just across the Chesapeake Bay.

Old Ben worked in the forests cutting timber. Old Rit worked for the Brodas family in their elegant mansion. Mr. Brodas bought and sold slaves the same way he did cattle and pigs. Old Ben and Old Rit had watched two of their daughters be sold to the Deep South. The couple grieved because they never saw the girls again. Little Harriet also saw her sisters being taken away in chains. The fear that she herself might be sold "down the river" never left her.

Little Harriet also heard the cries of slaves being whipped. The people around her were all very sad. "Why should such things be?" she wondered. "Is there no deliverance for my people?" Even as a child, she knew that **slavery** was not right.

The system of slavery separated not only children from their parents but also parents from each other. Slaves were not treated like people. They were property. Slaves often weren't allowed to marry. Even if a slave couple did get married, the husband could be hired out to another plantation at any time.

This drawing shows slaves during a rare moment of rest. They often had very little time off, poor food, and few clothes.

It was very rare for a slave child to live with both parents. Harriet felt lucky to have both her parents to watch over her and love her. The Ross cabin had floors of packed dirt. It didn't have windows. Light and air came in through the door. In the center of the cabin, an iron cooking pot hung over an open fire. They didn't have any furniture. The family slept on old rags. The master gave them very little food, mostly cheap salt pork, salt fish, cornmeal mush, and potatoes. As bare as the cabin was, it still made Harriet feel safe.

Harriet's work as a slave began when she was only six years old. Mr. Brodas hired her out to a family named Cook. Harriet was placed in a wagon driven by Mrs. Cook. No one told her what was happening. Then the wagon drove away.

Curled up on the floor of the wagon, Harriet began to cry. She wondered if she would ever see her mother and father again. Suddenly, she was hit on the neck. Mrs. Cook ordered Harriet to stop crying. It was Harriet's first taste of the cruelty of slavery, and it would not be her last.

Harriet had never been in a real house before. She had no idea what was expected of her. Sometimes she could not do what Mrs. Cook wanted her to do. Then she would feel the sting of the whip on her back. Mrs. Cook tried to put Harriet to work at the weaving loom. But no one told

Harriet how the loom worked and she couldn't do the job. She was whipped again.

When the day ended, Harriet hadn't finished her work. Mrs. Cook told the girl to rock the baby's cradle. The cradle was near Mrs. Cook's bed. If Harriet stopped rocking, Mrs. Cook snapped the whip at her. The scars that Mrs. Cook made on Harriet's neck stayed with her for the rest of her life.

At night Harriet slept on the kitchen floor. On the coldest nights she put her bare feet into the ashes of the dying fire to keep warm.

At last, Mrs. Cook saw that Harriet could not do housework. She turned the girl over to her husband. Mr. Cook put Harriet to work tending muskrat traps. Every day she waded for miles through icy creeks. She caught the measles and became very sick. The Cooks thought she was going to die. They sent her back home. They said that Harriet was too dumb to learn anything.

Back at the cabin, Old Rit used roots and herbs to nurse her daughter back to health. As soon as

Many slaves were cruelly beaten, as shown here. Harriet was often whipped as a child and never forgot the horrifying experiences.

she was able to work, Harriet was hired out again.

Harriet soon learned to trick the people she worked for. One mistress whipped Harriet almost every morning. So the girl dressed in extra layers of clothing to pad her back. She pretended that the beating hurt a lot. In the afternoon, she took off the heavy clothes.

Harriet did not make a good house slave. So she was put to work outside. She hauled wood and split rails. Working with other outdoor slaves, she learned the songs that had been sung by her people for generations. The **lyrics** held many hidden meanings. Code words told about escaping to freedom in the North.

One evening, Harriet was working late shucking corn. She saw a young slave slip away without asking permission. Curious, Harriet followed. The **overseer** caught up with the runaway slave. He threatened to tie up the runaway and whip him. The slave ran out of the store, right past Harriet.

The overseer yelled at Harriet to stop the man, but Harriet did nothing. Overcome with rage, the overseer picked up a two-pound lead weight from the scales and threw it at the man. The weight missed the man. Instead, it hit Harriet squarely on the head. Blood poured down her face. She fell to the floor unconscious.

No one thought Harriet would live. For days she lay on the floor of the old cabin. She didn't open her eyes. She didn't talk. The lead weight had pushed her skull against her brain. It left a scar that she would carry for the rest of her life.

No one called a doctor for slaves. Old Rit did the best she could with her herbal medicine.

Harriet's master tried to get rid of her, but no one wanted an injured slave. She would later recall, "They wouldn't give a sixpence for me."

Slowly, Harriet got better. But one thing had changed forever. Every so often, Harriet would drop off to sleep for 15 minutes or so. It didn't matter where she was or what she was doing. Nothing could wake her.

Slave owners chose husbands for the young slave girls. Not so with Harriet. Her owner thought she was crazy. Harriet often encouraged this thinking. She often pretended to have a **seizure** when white people were nearby.

Harriet prayed for her master's heart to change. "Oh, dear Lord," she said, "change [that] man's heart, and make him a Christian." But then she heard a rumor. As soon as she was able to move, she and her brother were going to be sold into a chain gang.

Harriet's prayer changed. "Lord, if you ain't never going to change [that] man's heart, *kill him, Lord,* and take him out of [the] way so he won't do more mischief."

Suddenly, Edward Brodas died. Harriet felt terrible. "I would give [the] world full of silver and gold, if I had it, to bring [that poor] soul back. I would give *myself.* I would give [everything]."

Harriet's religious **convictions** grew deeper. Praying wasn't something she did at a certain time. She had conversations with God all day long. The more she prayed, the more sure she became that she should not be a slave. Her mind was set on freedom.

This map of the Underground Railroad shows the routes slaves took to escape. Like many runaway slaves, Harriet risked her life and finally crossed the line to freedom.

2

Crossing the Line

Edward Brodas's son was too young to run the plantation when his father died. A **guardian** was called in to manage the affairs. Dr. Anthony Thompson became the supervisor.

Harriet convinced Thompson to hire her out to other farmers. She had to give most of her earnings to her master, but this arrangement gave her a bit more freedom. She was also able to save up a little money.

She was hired out to John Stewart. Stewart was a shipbuilder and timber operator. He was more fair than other men Harriet had worked for. Harriet's father also worked for Stewart cutting and hauling wood. Old Ben had become a valued worker.

Harriet grew to become very strong. She earned almost as much as a male slave. After several years of saving, she was able to purchase a yoke of oxen worth $40.

Working for Stewart also let her meet slaves from other areas. From them, she heard stories about the **Underground Railroad.** This was a network of people who helped slaves escape to the North.

The other slaves told stories of people who had escaped. They shared names of people who might help. They also told stories of those who didn't make it to freedom. These slaves were beaten and sold back into slavery. Harriet wanted to be free, but she knew it would not be easy.

When she tried to sleep, Harriet had nightmares. She saw "horsemen coming, and heard the shrieks of women and children, as they were being torn from each other, and hurried off no one knew whither." She was terrified of being sold down into the Deep South, where masters were known for treating their slaves even worse.

She also had another dream where she saw a line dividing the land of slavery from the land of freedom. On the other side of the line were lovely ladies dressed all in white. They waited to welcome her and care for her. Often she heard voices telling her to escape to freedom.

When Harriet was 24 years old, her master arranged for her to marry a free black man. His name was John Tubman. He lived in a cabin near the plantation. Marrying a free man did not change Harriet's status. She was still a slave. If she had any children, they too would become slaves.

Harriet often spoke to her husband about escaping to freedom. But John did not share her dreams. He ordered her to stop talking about such foolish things. He told her if she did plan an escape, he would tell on her. She learned to keep her dreams to herself. But she did not stop thinking about freedom.

The Brodas plantation was not doing well. The young master owed a lot of money. Then in 1849, he died. Rumor had it that the slaves would all be sold. Harriet talked with two of her brothers. The three of them decided to try to escape.

Harriet didn't want to leave without the rest of her family knowing what she was doing. She went to the big house where her sister was working. Slaves couldn't talk with each other when they were working. So Harriet used one of the songs she'd learned from the field workers. Drawing near the kitchen window, she sang:

> *I'll meet you in de mornin',*
> *When you reach de promised land;*
> *On the other side of Jordan,*
> *For I'm bound for the promised land.*

That night, Harriet waited for her husband to fall asleep. Then she slipped out to meet her brothers, and they started out. Pretty soon, fear gripped her two brothers. The North was far away. They might be caught. Then all kinds of terrible things could happen to them. Harriet's two brothers chose to turn back.

Harriet would do no such thing. "There was

In her escape to freedom, Harriet bravely traveled through the overgrown and dangerous swamps, like the slaves in this painting.

one of two things I had a right to, liberty, or death; if I could not have one, I would have [the other]; for no man should take me alive."

She set out alone. She didn't have a map. At night, her guide was the North Star. During the day, she noted the moss growing on the north sides of the trees. She had heard from the other slaves about following the Choptank River. The river led to the Chesapeake Bay. There, a runaway could follow the water highway north to Baltimore, then Delaware, and on to Philadelphia. Harriet chose the land route.

She got some help from the Underground Railroad. Even so, she had to be very careful, hiding her tracks and staying away from roads. Slave owners and slave hunters were afraid to walk through the swamps. Harriet was not. She traveled at night and slept in hiding places during the day. Before long, she became very aware of danger. She could sense danger before most other people did.

After many days, she made it to Wilmington, Delaware. It was just a short distance from the border of Pennsylvania. That border was the line she had seen in her dreams so many times. **Abolitionists** in Wilmington helped Harriet. They told her how she would know when she was in Pennsylvania. Once she reached that state, she would be in free land.

Harriet never forgot that wonderful moment when she crossed the dividing line between slavery and freedom. "I looked at my hands to see if I was the same person now [that] I was free," she wrote. "There was such a glory over everything. The sun came like gold through the trees and over the fields, and I felt like I was in heaven."

Her dream had really come true. The city of Philadelphia boasted the largest black community in the country at that time. Harriet looked for a job. Hard work was nothing new to her, so she worked many jobs. Now the money was hers to keep. But she could not enjoy spending it on herself. She longed to have her family with her. She could not enjoy her freedom while others were still in **bondage**.

Harriet knew that her family would not try to escape on their own. There was only one answer. She would save her money. Then she would go back to the South and bring the others out. Over the next 10 years, this plan would make her a legend.

White abolitionists help runaway slaves reach the safety of an Underground Railroad station. Harriet became friendly with white pastors and Quakers who helped slaves escape from the South.

3

Conductor on the Underground Railroad

In 1850, blacks in America were filled with terror. Congress passed a law called the **Fugitive** Slave Act. Under this law, any black person could be charged with being a runaway. It didn't matter if they were slave or free. Then they would be brought before a judge. No black person was allowed a jury trial. They couldn't speak for themselves. It also became against the law to help a runaway slave.

The law made many Northerners angry. They watched as black people were marched through their streets in chains. They decided to do something about slavery. Many stood ready to spend their money to help

In February 1839, some slave traders kidnapped some Africans and sailed to Cuba. Spanish planters bought 53 of the men and put them aboard the *Amistad*. The Africans seized control of the ship and demanded to be returned to Africa. Then a U.S. navy ship took over the *Amistad*. The Africans were put in prison. Some died there.

Soon everyone was fighting over these men. Finally, the case went to the Supreme Court. The Court decided that the Africans should go home. In January 1841, the men who were still alive went back to Africa.

free slaves. Some of them even risked their lives. Many of these people joined the Underground Railroad. A white **clergyman** named James Miller McKim and a free black man named William Still decided to help. They joined a group of people in Philadelphia who worked for the Underground Railroad.

Harriet became close friends with both Pastor McKim and Mr. Still. Because the work was dangerous, few people kept records of what they were doing. But Still wrote down what he heard from the runaway slaves. He hid these records in a nearby graveyard. Years later, his writings provided some of the only evidence of Harriet's work with the Underground Railroad.

Slave auctions were common in small towns like this. Harriet's own sister was rescued from an auction block and hidden by Quakers.

Harriet's first trip took place in December 1850. Her sister Mary Ann was married to a free black man named John Bowley. He contacted the Railroad. He wanted help getting his family out of slavery. Harriet found out that they needed help. She said that if Bowley could get his family as far as Baltimore, she could take them to Philadelphia.

The plan nearly fell through. Mary Ann's master suddenly took her and the children to the auction block to be sold. Bowley went to the auction. He claimed to be a slave belonging to the auctioneer. He gave the guard an official-looking letter. It asked that the female captive and her children be released to go with Bowley. The guard did as he was asked.

Quickly John took his family to the safety of a **Quaker** home. They hid in the attic until night. Under cover of darkness, they took a sailboat north. Finally, they saw flashing lantern lights sending a coded message and they went ashore.

Quakers Levi and Catharine Coffin were famous for helping thousands of slaves escape to freedom. Levi was often called the president of the Underground Railroad.

Their eight-room house in Newport, Indiana, was built in 1839. It provided a place of safety for the fugitives. They could hide runaways in their home for several weeks. This gave the slaves a chance to get strong enough for the rest of the journey. Every slave who came to the Coffin house made it to freedom.

There they were met by other Quakers. These people hid John and his family in a potato wagon. The wagon drove to a home. Waiting for them was Harriet. She guided them the rest of the way to safety.

This was the first of 19 journeys Harriet made into slave areas. Eventually she helped more than 300 slaves escape. She later said, "I never ran my train off the track, and I never lost a passenger."

The next year, Harriet was ready to help free her brother John Ross, who was working in Maryland. Harriet helped John and two other men escape to freedom.

Harriet began thinking about her husband. Getting him out of the South would be much more dangerous. She would have to go back to the place where many people knew her. She decided it was worth the risk.

Harriet faced terrible danger for nothing. John Tubman had no interest in leaving. Harriet found out that he had married a new wife. This news hurt her very much. But she lost no time in finding others to take the trip to freedom. On her way home, she brought 10 slaves to the North.

Harriet never said much about John Tubman after this trip. She did not let disappointment slow her down. She would help any slave who was willing to take the dangerous journey to freedom.

Sometimes the groups were quite large. Other times they were small. Rescuing slaves was like running a war. It called for leadership skills and strict discipline. Early on, Harriet came up with a method that carried her through years of rescue work. She always started out with her group on Saturday night. That way they would not be missed until Monday morning. It gave them two nights to get away.

Sometimes signs about the missing slaves were posted in the towns ahead of them. Harriet hired someone to take them down as quickly as they were put up.

Her strong body allowed her to put up with the hard travel. They climbed mountains, crossed rivers, and pushed through thick forests. Her

Harriet helped over 300 runaway slaves escape to freedom, like the ones in this painting. Amazingly, she never used a map.

group endured all types of weather.

Many who traveled with her dropped from exhaustion. They cried that they could not take another step. Out came Harriet's gun. Pointing it at the person's head, she would say, "You go on or die!" This forced each slave to keep moving no matter how tired they were.

Would she really have killed someone who gave up? She responded, "Yes. If he was weak enough to give out, he'd be weak enough to betray us all. . . . Do you think I'd let so many die just for one coward man?" Thankfully, she never had to use the gun. Later, those she threatened with death thanked her for being tough with them. Her toughness saved their lives.

When necessary, Harriet would use a different route. She knew which towns were the safest and which she should avoid at all costs. One time she left her charges in the woods and entered a town. She knocked on the door where her contact lived. A stranger answered the door. He said the other person had been forced to leave. Harriet knew she had brought attention to herself. Remembering a swamp outside of town, she led her group into the tall, wet grass. There they hid in the cold. Harriet prayed for help.

After dusk that evening, a man in Quaker dress

came walking along near the swamp. He seemed to be talking to himself. "My wagon stands in the barnyard of the next farm across the way. The horse is in the stable. The harness hangs on a nail."

This man was the answer to Harriet's prayer. When darkness fell, she made her way to the barn and found the wagon stocked with provisions. Hitching up the horse, she carried her group to the next station.

Harriet received help from many people. Thomas Garrett owned a store in Wilmington. He gave both goods from his store and money to help the slaves. He didn't hide what he was doing. Enemies watched him closely. The free blacks watched closely as well, and

Thomas Garrett's hardware store was a busy stop on the Underground Railroad. Two times, he was charged with helping slaves escape. He paid such big fines that he lost all his money. But he never stopped helping slaves.

He was arrested again and the judge said, "Garrett, let this be a lesson to you, not to interfere."

Garrett answered, "Judge, thee hasn't left me a dollar, but I wish to say . . . that if anyone knows of a fugitive who wants a shelter and a friend, send him to Thomas Garrett, and he will befriend him!"

This drawing of Harriet, or "Moses" as she was often called, shows her as a strong, fearless woman.

often warned him of danger.

In 1857, Garrett received a letter from many people in Scotland with money to help Harriet's work. By that time, she was well-known. Garrett had not heard from Harriet for several days. At last, she appeared in his office. She told him that God had sent her to pick up her money. Teasing her, Garrett offered her a new pair of shoes instead. She answered, "You can give me what I need, now. God never fools me."

Garrett asked if anyone had told her about the money. "No, nobody but God," she answered. The amount Garrett held for her was the exact amount she needed at the moment.

Harriet worked during the winter and summer. This earned her enough money to travel to the South in the spring and fall. Throughout the South, Harriet became known as "Moses." Some slave owners refused to believe she was a woman. They thought that only a man could be so daring and courageous. She made use of that idea when she disguised herself. She often dressed as a man or a stooped-shouldered old woman.

In the first few trips, Harriet brought her groups as far as Philadelphia. But the Fugitive

Slave Act made even Philadelphia dangerous. She started taking her groups all the way up to Canada.

Just before Christmas in 1854, Harriet started to worry about her three brothers who were still in Maryland. She didn't usually travel in winter, but Harriet learned her brothers were to be sold soon.

Secretly, Harriet sent word to the three men to meet her in a loft near their parents' cabin. Harriet had not seen her mother for more than six years. She didn't dare let the woman know she was coming. Her mother might try to stop them.

Old Ben brought them food. He kept his eyes covered with a rag. Later when he was questioned, he could honestly say he had *seen* no one.

Harriet stole up to the little cabin. She saw Old Rit sitting in her rocking chair with her head in her hands. The old woman was sad because her sons hadn't come for Christmas dinner. Harriet wept as she watched her mother. Then she turned sadly away.

By daybreak, she and her brothers and three other runaways were safe at the first Underground Railroad stop.

About two years later, Harriet went back for her parents. They would not be sold because they were too old. But Harriet learned that Old Ben was suspected of helping runaways. He was charged and was to appear in court. Harriet arrived the day before Ben was to be tried. She knew her parents could not walk. With the help of friends, she constructed a "freedom chariot." Taking two wheels and an axle from a cast-off buggy, she placed a board across the axle where her parents could sit. Another board gave a place for them to rest their feet. She then rounded up an old horse and made a harness. Riding all night, they reached southern Delaware by morning. From there, she led her elderly parents to freedom in Canada.

By the end of the 1850s, Harriet had helped all of her family escape except for one sister and her children. Because of her success, slave owners hated Harriet. They offered a $12,000 reward for her capture. Harriet trusted that God would take care of her.

This painting shows a flood of runaway slaves, which meant huge financial losses for Southerners. The South got ready to go to war with the North in part because of the issue of slavery.

Active
Abolitionist

Southerners faced a big problem. In 1850, about 50,000 escaped slaves lived in the North. They were worth more than $15 million to their owners. More slaves escaped every day. Without slaves, Southerners might not be able to run their plantations. Their way of life would end.

This fear led to tougher laws in the Southern states. These laws gave long prison sentences to any person handing out books or newspapers that might encourage the slaves to revolt.

In 1852, Harriet Beecher Stowe wrote a book entitled *Uncle Tom's Cabin*. The book illustrated what was wrong with slavery. It hit the nation by storm. Before the year was out, a million copies had been sold.

The book made people in the South very angry. In many areas, the book was **banned.** The Reverend Samuel Green was a free black man who lived in Maryland. He got into trouble for owning a copy of the book. He was sent to prison for 10 years.

In the North, more people began to take action against slavery. A play based on the story of Uncle Tom appeared in theaters in every major city.

Friends of Harriet Tubman invited her to join them to see the play. She answered, "I've heard *Uncle Tom's Cabin* read and I tell you, Mrs. Stowe's pen hasn't begun to paint what slavery is. . . . I've seen the real thing and I don't want to see it on any stage."

As the possibility of war between the North and the South grew more likely, Harriet kept making trips into slave states to free people. But she also became more involved in the abolitionist movement. She met with some of the most important people in the nation.

Two of those people were William H. Seward and his wife. The Sewards lived in Auburn, New York. They became good friends with Harriet. Mr. Seward had been governor of New York State. In 1848, he became a U.S. senator. He argued against the Fugitive Slave Law.

Seward introduced Harriet to Frederick Douglass, who was also a runaway slave from Maryland. Douglass was editor of his own abolitionist newspaper called the _North Star_.

Harriet often stayed at the home of the Douglasses when passing through New York on her way to Canada. Douglass was an active part of the Underground Railroad. Other times, Harriet stayed at the home of Susan B. Anthony. This woman was fighting for women's rights.

Yet another abolitionist friend was millionaire Gerrit Smith. His father had been a partner with the wealthy John Jacob Astor. While she was at Mr. Smith's home, Harriet met another woman who fought for women's rights. Her name was Elizabeth Cady Stanton.

Everyone loved hearing Harriet's stories. She always used little jokes in her stories to keep people interested. Harriet was very busy. She didn't have a lot of time to give speeches. She had to work as a maid to support herself. She never got paid for giving a speech, like Frederick Douglass did. But that didn't keep her from talking at meetings whenever someone asked her to. One newspaper account said that "she used rolling words that were colorful and biting."

A pastor named Thomas Wentworth Higginson also worked to end slavery. People thought he was one of the best speakers of his day. He praised Harriet's speaking ability. He said that he learned to speak by listening to people like Harriet Tubman.

Writing to his mother, Higginson said, "We have had the greatest heroine of the age here, Harriet Tubman, a black woman and a fugitive slave." He went on to describe the great reward

Frederick Douglass was also a runaway slave. Like Harriet, he often spoke out against slavery.

offered for her capture. Then he added, "[She] will probably be burned alive whenever she is caught."

It was Harriet's close friendship with the abolitionists that led to her 1858 meeting with John Brown. Brown was very blunt about his feelings against slavery. Early in his life, he had dedicated himself to bringing an end to slavery in the nation.

When Kansas became a state, the people who lived there were supposed to decide whether slavery would be allowed. People in favor of slavery rushed into the state. They wanted to force the people of Kansas to vote for slavery.

Abolitionists decided to do the same thing. They paid John Brown and other men to go to Kansas and work to keep slavery out of the state. The fight started with words, but it ended in violence. Because of this the state earned the nickname "Bloody Kansas."

These happenings did not surprise Harriet. She had always said that the end of slavery would not come peacefully.

When Harriet was introduced to John Brown, they had both heard of each other.

This most wonderful woman — Harriet Tubman — is still alive — I saw her but the other day at the beautiful home of Eliza Wright Osborne — the daughter of Martha C. Wright — in company with Elizabeth Smith Miller — the only daughter of Gerrit Smith — Miss Emily Howland — her niece Mrs. Shaw — and Mrs. Ella Wright Garrison — the daughter of Martha C. Wright and the wife of Wm Lloyd Garrison Jr — all of us were visiting at the Osbornes — a real love feast of the few that are left — and here came Harriet Tubman!

Susan B. Anthony
Jan. 6 1903. *17 Madison Street*
Rochester — N.Y.

In this 1903 letter, Susan B. Anthony, a women's rights activist, talked about Harriet and the fact that she was still alive and active at age 82.

John Brown shook Harriet's hand three times. As he did, he said, "The first I see is General Tubman, the second is General Tubman, and the third is General Tubman." From then on, he never referred to Harriet as anything but General Tubman.

Harriet thought a great deal of John Brown as well. She had never met a white man who was so dedicated to freeing blacks. At the time, John Brown was forming a plan for a huge slave rebellion. He wanted to form a series of Underground Railroad stations in the mountains of Virginia. From those stations, he would attack nearby plantations. They would then free the slaves.

Harriet told him what she knew of safe contacts in the area. She also explained what the area looked like. She agreed to get freed men in who would help. She also helped to raise money. A committee of abolitionists who gathered to help John Brown became known as the "secret six."

Then their support began to weaken. John Brown changed his plans. He decided to attack the federal arsenal at Harpers Ferry, Virginia.

This was a place where weapons were stored. He thought that once they seized the arms at the arsenal, slaves would flee from their masters and join him in the mountains.

Meanwhile, Harriet was taking care of her parents. The old couple did not do well during the cold winters in Canada. They needed to be moved. William Seward helped Harriet buy a home in Auburn, New York, so her parents could live there. Harriet was busy getting furniture for the house. Then she moved them to New York. After that, she had to work very hard to pay bills and support her family.

When John Brown sent word for her to come help with the attack, Harriet could not be found. The great general had fallen ill from working too hard. She lay in a friend's cottage in New Bedford, Massachusetts, so sick that she could even not think or talk.

John Brown's attack at Harpers Ferry was not successful. Many men were killed during the fight. John Brown was captured, and later put to

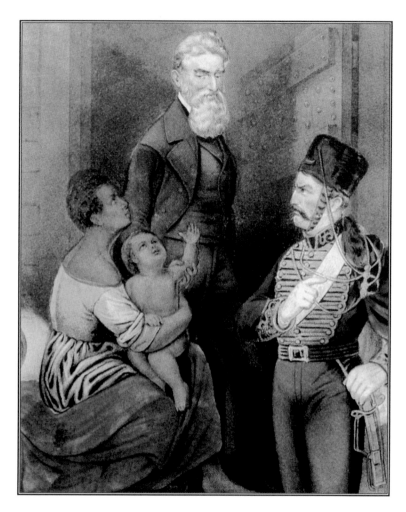

A soldier takes John Brown to jail. Brown also fought to end slavery, but unlike Harriet, he was willing to use violence.

death. Had it not been for her illness, Harriet might have been at the battle and killed as well. She was very sad to learn that John Brown was dead. For the rest of her life she called him "John Brown, my dearest friend."

In April 1860, Harriet was staying with a relative in Troy, New York. Word came that a slave had been captured and was to appear in court. Donning a shawl and bonnet, Harriet hurried toward the court. She asked for help from the black community as she went.

The slave, Charles Nalle, was one-eighth black. His father was his white master, and his mother was only one-quarter black. Nalle himself was very light-skinned. But none of that mattered. He was a slave and the property of his owner.

Harriet, looking like a stooped old lady, made her way up the stairs to where the man was being held. Officers held Nalle with chains on his wrists. As they began leading the man down the stairs, Harriet attacked. She wrestled the man away from the officers. Then she almost dragged him down the stairs.

Police beat her with clubs. They knocked her

to the ground again and again. Harriet hung on to Nalle tightly. She never let go of her grip on the slave.

The street swarmed with people who wanted to help Nalle. They grabbed him and loaded him into a wagon. Eventually the black man made his way to freedom. Harriet also escaped and went into hiding. A few months later, the community of Troy raised money and bought Nalle's freedom.

Stories like this made Harriet a folk hero. They also made people in the North and South more angry with each other.

Harriet was in even more danger now. She was well-known all over the nation. But she decided to make one more trip to Maryland. She wanted to try to find her sister and bring her to the North. However, once she reached Maryland, Harriet learned that her sister had died. She brought out seven other slaves instead.

In 1860, Abraham Lincoln was elected

president. People in the South were upset. Several Southern states broke away from the Union. **Compromises** were presented to Congress by people who hoped to keep the nation from war.

Harriet told a friend, "They may say, 'Peace! Peace!' as much as they like. I know there's going to be war!"

As usual, "Moses" was right.

This picture shows Harriet around the time of the Civil War. She went on many dangerous missions and bravely served the Union throughout the war.

General Tubman Serves Her Country

The Civil War began in April 1861. Southern troops fired on Fort Sumter in South Carolina. News this important traveled very quickly. Harriet was in Canada at the time, but she soon learned what had happened and hurried back to the United States. She was ready to serve her country.

But first she had to find someone who believed that a 40-year-old black woman belonged in the Union army. Through her abolitionist friends, she was put in touch with John A. Andrew. He was the governor of Massachusetts and a strong abolitionist.

Andrew sent Harriet to South Carolina near

Fort Sumter sits on an island near South Carolina. The Confederates had stored guns and cannons around it. They planned on taking it away from the Union.

The battle began on April 12, 1861. The Confederates fired 3,341 times in 33 hours. The barracks of the fort were in ruins. The main gate was gone.

On April 14, Union Major Robert Anderson and his men surrendered. The Union flag was shot full of holes. Four years later, Anderson returned as a general to take back the fort. He raised the same Union flag over Fort Sumter.

where the Union troops were blocking off Charleston Harbor. Union troops had taken over some of the islands. Most of the people who owned the plantations on the islands had run away. They left their slaves behind.

Harriet's job was to report to the Union army and help these abandoned blacks. The slaves were called "**contraband** of war." They were not legally free, but they were also no longer slaves.

The slaves around Beaufort, South Carolina, spoke a special language that contained many African words. Harriet didn't understand much of what they said. This made it harder to work with them.

Harriet had to win their trust little by little. She could get food from the army because of her job. She chose not to because she didn't want the released slaves to be jealous of her. At night, she made pies and root beer and sold them to make her own living.

Harriet was busy finding much-needed clothing and supplies for the freed slaves. Then she tried to help them find work to do. At one point she built a washhouse and taught many of the women how to earn a living by doing laundry for the soldiers. She also worked as a nurse in a big house that was being used as a hospital. Harriet remembered what her mother had done with herbs to help sick people. She used that knowledge to help the blacks who were hurt and ill. She helped the wounded soldiers as well.

Harriet continued to move from place to place, doing whatever she could to help other people. In Florida she treated soldiers who were suffering from smallpox and malaria. She never got any of those diseases herself, however. Sarah Bradford, a woman who would later write Harriet's story, noted that the "general" had little fear of dying. She believed that God would take good care of her until it was her time to go.

Harriet worked extremely hard for the Union. But she did not always completely agree with how President Lincoln chose to handle things. She felt he was taking far too much time in freeing the slaves. She believed the war should bring freedom to her people immediately. In January 1863, Harriet was overjoyed at receiving some very good news. President Lincoln had finally issued the **Emancipation Proclamation.** Once and for all, it gave freedom to all slaves.

Governor Andrew said that Harriet would make a good spy. She could go behind enemy lines and get information. She had lots of practice acting out different roles and wearing disguises. She also had many contacts from

During the war, Harriet trained freed slave women to do laundry and other household chores so they could make a living.

her work with the Underground Railroad. So
Harriet was sent on dangerous missions. Each
time, when she returned, she remembered the

smallest details about each route. This helped Union officers make much better plans.

One day during the war, Harriet Tubman helped a slave woman with two pigs get aboard a boat. Harriet's arms were full, and she tripped on her long skirt and nearly tore it off. She decided that she needed a real uniform.

Harriet got a coat and dress in federal blue. She wore a bandanna over her hair. Her satchel was filled with first-aid supplies. Then she added something special. She got a pair of "bloomers" (a style of pants made for women by a woman named Amelia Bloomer). From then on, Harriet proudly wore her bloomers on every trip.

Later that same year, Harriet was asked to head up a scouting service. She selected many other scouts who would also take on dangerous missions and go behind enemy lines. These scouts got a great deal of information for many different Union generals. Wherever she and her workers had spied, the Union troops were able to plan and stage more successful attacks.

The officers invited Harriet to go with them as they launched attacks against many large plantations along the Combahee River. They burned crops and destroyed buildings. Hundreds of freed slaves were found hiding in terror. They had been told by their owners that the Yankees were mean and cruel and that they had horns. Harriet's presence helped ease those fears. Often she would sing to calm them down. One time, she sang a very old spiritual. Only this time, she made up new words for it:

> *Come along! Come along! Don't be a fool,*
> *Uncle Sam's rich enough to send us all to school!*

Many of these freed slaves joined the Union army. The first black troops had arrived from Massachusetts. They included the two sons of Frederick Douglass. Harriet knew many of the soldiers and their officers. She stayed with them for quite a while. She cooked, did laundry, and carried messages for them.

During the summer of 1863, Harriet also took part in a famous raid. She stood beside Colonel Patrick Montgomery and watched 150 black soldiers board each of three gunboats.

President Lincoln and his cabinet read the proposed Emancipation Proclamation. Harriet felt the president had taken far too long to free the slaves, and that their freedom should be a natural result of the war.

The boats headed up the Combahee River. There, they destroyed millions of dollars worth of Confederate supplies and freed nearly 800 slaves. Not one man was killed.

Harriet respected Montgomery. But she was disappointed when he received all the credit for the success of the raid. In a letter to a friend, she said, "Don't you think we colored people are entitled to some of the credit for that exploit, under the lead of the brave Colonel Montgomery?"

By this time, Harriet had been away from her parents for two long years. She could only hope her neighbors were taking care of the older couple. She worried about them but did not see how she could leave the important work she was doing.

In July 1863, Harriet was witness to another big event. A black unit called the 54th Massachusetts attacked Fort Wagner. The men were led by Robert Gould Shaw. This was the first battle in which black troops fought. Many white people thought black men would run from battle. Even though they lost the battle, the soldiers proved these people were wrong. Their leader Colonel Shaw was killed. But the black soldiers didn't run away. After the battle at Fort Wagner, black soldiers were often used in battle.

By 1865, Harriet had grown tired. She asked if she could go see her parents and get some rest. The army said she could.

Back home in New York, Harriet was very sick. She didn't sleep well. Kind neighbors often brought her food. One of the people who visited Harriet was Sarah Hopkins Bradford. Sarah was the daughter of a professor at the Auburn Theological Seminary. Sarah Bradford had often cared for Harriet's parents. She had written letters to their daughter for them. As Harriet got better, Sarah listened to her stories and decided to write some of them down. After the war, these stories were included in a book called *Scenes in the Life of Harriet Tubman.*

By the spring of 1865, Harriet felt well enough to travel once again. She wanted to return to South Carolina. But by the time she arrived in Washington, D.C., a series of Union victories had turned

Colonel Shaw leads his black troops in the attack on Fort Wagner. Even though they lost the battle, the black troops proved that they could do well in combat.

the tide of war. On April 9, the largest Southern army surrendered. Just a week later, President Lincoln was killed by an assassin's bullet.

Jefferson Davis was the only president of the Confederate States of America. He grew up on a Mississippi plantation. He studied and trained at West Point.

Later, he served in the U.S. government. He was a senator when Mississippi left the Union in January 1861. The Southern states chose him to be president of their new nation.

When the South lost the war, Davis still urged Southerners to keep fighting. He was captured and spent two years in prison. He died in New Orleans in 1889.

After the war was over, Harriet worked for a while as a nurse in Fort Monroe, Virginia. As bad as things had been in South Carolina at the beginning of the war, Fort Monroe was much worse. She did what she could to make things better. Then she felt her war work was finished.

In spite of all her hard work, Harriet never got paid by the government. She turned in a number of expense receipts, but the government ignored her requests for back pay. Payment to any black person was a new idea for the time. White people had a hard time thinking of paying black men for their work. Black soldiers were paid less than half the salary of white soldiers. But to pay a black *woman* was too much to take in.

Tired and poor, Harriet hopped aboard a northbound train. She carried her government pass for half fare. The conductor did not believe a black woman could possibly be a government employee. He told her she would have to ride in the baggage car. Harriet refused to move. It took three men to remove her from the car and throw her into the baggage car. In the struggle, her shoulder was hurt.

The woman who had been so willing to give her life for her country was riding home in a baggage car. Where was the freedom she'd fought so hard to preserve?

After the war Harriet retired to a small town in upstate New York, like this one. She continued to work for women's rights and was even honored by the queen of England.

6

Swing Low, Sweet Chariot

Harriet did not sit around and feel sorry for herself. She went right to work at her home in Auburn, New York. She planted a large garden to feed herself, her family, and friends. She also hired herself out as a nurse, a cleaning lady, and a nanny.

Money was always in short supply. Whatever she made, Harriet usually gave away. She helped support her parents, who lived to be nearly 100 years old. She also helped a brother, a grandniece, and a nephew.

People who had heard of "Moses" tried to find her. Some were poor, wandering blacks who had no idea how to support themselves. Some were sick.

Others were just old and tired. Harriet never turned anyone away.

A different type of stranger came to her door in 1869. Nelson Davis was a young black man whom Harriet had nursed back to health during the war. He was just 20 years old, and Harriet was 49. Despite their age difference, the two were married on March 18, 1869. It was later learned that Nelson was sick with tuberculosis. During the 19 years he and Harriet were married, Nelson never worked. That meant Harriet had another mouth to feed.

In her later years, Harriet kept fighting for women's rights. She remained close friends with the women who led that battle. In 1897, a group of women in Boston gave a party in Harriet's honor. Someone asked Harriet if she truly believed that women should have the right to vote. She answered, "I suffered enough to believe it."

After the Civil War, stories about the daring Underground Railroad could finally be made public. Sarah Bradford helped Harriet pay for her house by writing a book about Harriet's trips to the South.

Bradford asked rich people like Gerrit Smith to help pay for the printing. The book became very popular.

Other reporters and writers were struck by Harriet's many stories. They visited her in her home and listened to every word she said. William Wells Brown included "Moses" in his book *The Rising Son.* "Moses had no education," he wrote, "yet the most refined person would listen for hours while she related the intensely interesting incidents of her life, told in the simplest manner, but always seasoned with good sense."

Nelson died in 1888. Harriet then received a widow's pension of eight dollars a month. She was paid for being the widow of a man who had fought in the Civil War. But she was never paid for her own brave service.

Harriet was honored by the queen of England, however. After reading Bradford's book about Harriet, Queen Victoria sent a silver medal and a silk shawl to the former slave. She invited her to come to England in 1897. Had she been younger, Harriet might have made that trip. She showed the letter from the queen to so many people that it was nearly worn to shreds.

Even as she was growing old, Harriet dreamed of building a home for other old, poor, and homeless blacks. Through the money she earned from the second edition of her book, and with contributions from her neighbors, she began the work. In 1896, she was able to buy 25 acres of land next to her own home. Later, she deeded the land to the African Methodist Episcopal Zion Church, which she attended.

Harriet was thrilled to see the home completed in 1908. But she was upset that the church chose to charge residents to move in. She wanted the home to be free to anyone who needed a place to stay. "What's the good of a Home," she asked, "if a person who wants to get in has to have money?" She and the church leaders eventually reached a compromise on the issue.

Harriet moved into the home in 1911. Early in 1913, she became ill with pneumonia. When she died on March 10, a number of her friends who

Harriet died surrounded by friends. Her funeral was attended by most of the town and many important people from all over the country.

were there surrounded her bed and sang her favorite spiritual, "Swing Low, Sweet Chariot."

Nearly all of the city of Auburn turned out for her funeral. Booker T. Washington, a respected black leader, spoke at the memorial service. He said Harriet was the woman who "made it possible for the white race to place a

This monument to Harriet Tubman in Boston honors her many years of service in the fight for freedom.

higher estimate upon the black race."

Harriet Tubman was keenly aware that no one had *given* her freedom to her. She had *taken* her own freedom in a movement unlike any our country has ever known before or since.

GLOSSARY

abolitionist–a person who works to get rid of slavery

ban–to prevent the use of by law

bondage–the state of being under the power of another, as in slavery

clergyman–a pastor or preacher

compromise–an agreement between two sides in which each side gives up some of its claims

contraband–goods that have been seized or taken

conviction–a strong belief

Emancipation Proclamation–the formal freeing of slaves in the United States

fugitive–a person who flees; a runaway

guardian–one who takes care of the person or property of another

lyrics–the words of a song

overseer–a person who watches over, supervises, or inspects

plantation–a large estate or farm on which crops are grown and harvested by workers who live there

Quaker–member of the Society of Friends, a Christian group, who are against slavery and violence

seizure–an attack or fit in which the body loses control

slavery–when one person is owned by another person

Underground Railroad–a network of places and people helping slaves escape to freedom

CHRONOLOGY

1820	Born Harriet Ross on the Brodas plantation in Maryland.
1835	Is hit on the head with a lead weight resulting in a life-long problem of "sleeping fits."
1844	Marries John Tubman.
1849	Escapes to the North.
1850	Makes the first trip back into Maryland to bring more slaves to freedom.
1857	Rescues her parents from slavery; begins living in Auburn, New York.
1858	Meets and befriends John Brown.
1861	Launches into war work serving as nurse and aiding the wounded on both sides.
1863	Serves as a spy for the Union army; leads a raid into South Carolina.
1869	Marries Nelson Davis.
1888	Nelson Davis dies.
1897	Is awarded a medal from Queen Victoria of England.
1908	Builds a home for old, sick, and homeless blacks.
1911	Moves into the home.
1913	Dies of pneumonia at age 93.

CIVIL WAR TIME LINE

1860   Abraham Lincoln is elected president of the United States on November 6. During the next few months, Southern states begin to break away from the Union.

1861   On April 12, the Confederates attack Fort Sumter, South Carolina, and the Civil War begins. Union forces are defeated in Virginia at the First Battle of Bull Run (First Manassas) on July 21 and withdraw to Washington, D.C.

1862   Robert E. Lee is placed in command of the main Confederate army in Virginia in June. Lee defeats the Army of the Potomac at the Second Battle of Bull Run (Second Manassas) in Virginia on August 29–30. On September 17, Union general George B. McClellan turns back Lee's first invasion of the North at Antietam Creek near Sharpsburg, Maryland. It is the bloodiest day of the war.

1863   On January 1, President Lincoln issues the Emancipation Proclamation, freeing slaves in Southern states. Between May 1–6, Lee wins an important victory at Chancellorsville, but key Southern commander Thomas J. "Stonewall" Jackson dies from wounds. In June, Union forces hold the city of Vicksburg, Mississippi, under siege. The people of Vicksburg surrender on July 4. Lee's second invasion of the North during July 1–3 is decisively turned back at Gettysburg, Pennsylvania.

1864   General Grant is made supreme Union commander on March 9. Following a series of costly battles, on June 19 Grant successfully encircles Lee's troops in Petersburg, Virginia. A siege of the town lasts nearly a year. Union general William Sherman captures Atlanta on September 2 and begins the "March to the Sea," a campaign of destruction across Georgia and South Carolina. On November 8, Abraham Lincoln wins reelection as president.

1865   On April 2, Petersburg, Virginia, falls to the Union. Lee attempts to reach Confederate forces in North Carolina but is gradually surrounded by Union troops. Lee surrenders to Grant on April 9 at Appomattox, Virginia, ending the war. Abraham Lincoln is assassinated by John Wilkes Booth on April 14.

FURTHER READING

Bial, Raymond. *The Underground Railroad*. New York: Houghton Mifflin, 1999.

Edwards, Pamela Duncan. *Barefoot: Escape on the Underground Railroad*. New York: HarperCollins, 1997.

Greenwood, Barbara. *The Last Safe House: A Story of the Underground Railroad*. Buffalo, N.Y.: Kids Can Press, 1998.

Johnston, Norma. *Over Jordan*. New York: Avon Camelot, 1999.

Lutz, Norma Jean. *Escape from Slavery*. Philadelphia: Chelsea House, 2000.

Taylor, M. W. *Harriet Tubman*. Philadelphia: Chelsea House, 1991.

INDEX

PICTURE CREDITS

page

ABOUT THE AUTHOR

NORMA JEAN LUTZ lives in Tulsa, Oklahoma. She has been writing professionally since 1977. She is the author of more than 250 short stories and articles, as well as more than 40 books–fiction and nonfiction. Of all the writing she does, she most enjoys writing children's books.

Senior Consulting Editor **ARTHUR M. SCHLESINGER, JR.** is the leading American historian of our time. He won the Pulitzer Prize for his book *The Age of Jackson* (1945), and again for *A Thousand Days* (1965). This chronicle of the Kennedy Administration also won a National Book Award. He has written many other books, including a multi-volume series, *The Age of Roosevelt.* Professor Schlesinger is the Albert Schweitzer Professor of the Humanities at the City University of New York, and has been involved in several other Chelsea House projects, including the COLONIAL LEADERS series of biographies on the most prominent figures of early American history.